AN INTRODUCTION TO
GRAND CANYON
PREHISTORY

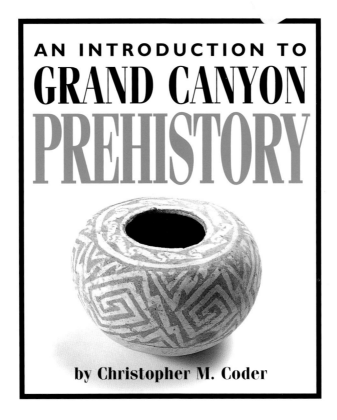

by Christopher M. Coder

Grand Canyon Association
Grand Canyon, Arizona

Copyright 2000 Grand Canyon Association
Revised 2006
Post Office Box 399, Grand Canyon, Arizona 86023
928.638.2481
www.grandcanyon.org

ISBN: 0-938216-70-8

Library of Congress Card Catalog Number: 99-75383

10 9 8 7 6 5

Project Manager: L. Greer Price

Editorial: Sandra Scott

Book Design: Christina Watkins

Book Typography and Production: Triad Associates

Production Supervisor: Kimberly Buchheit

Printed in Singapore on recycled paper.

Grand Canyon Association is a not-for-profit organization. Net proceeds from the sale of this book will be used to support the educational goals of Grand Canyon National Park.

Acknowledgments

Any interest generated by this book is the result of a team effort due in large part to the talents and vision of my editor, Sandra Scott, and our graphic designer, Christina Watkins. I extend my personal gratitude to my wife, Marcelle, and to Greer Price of Grand Canyon Association for their support. A special thanks to NPS archaeologist Jan Balsom and her staff, and to the staff of Special Collections, Cline Library. To my friends and colleagues who in various ways added to the experience: Jim Huffman, Phil Geib, Robert Euler, Joe Pachak, Man Susanyatame, Loretta Jackson, Leigh Kuwanwisiwma, Winston Hurst, Jonathan Till, Duane Hubbard, Mike Quinn, Melissa Schroeder, Joe Dista, Ivo Lucchitta, Angie Bullets, Richard Stoffle, Henry Lane, Roger Echo Hawk, Rex Tilousi, Debbie Westfall, Mark Bond, Bill Davis, Christine Goetze, David Wilcox, Pete Bungart, Victoria Clark, Helen Fairley and Lynden Murray; to Mark Taylor and J.E. Whipp Jr. for their inspiration; and to my boatmen Deb Peterson, John Davenport, Deutschlander, Tamara and Dave Desrosiers, Lisa Whisnant, Dave "Big Wave" Christiansen, Grusy, Gidget Rivers, Ed "Participate..." Smith, Jon Hirsch, Kenton Grua, Thud, Brian Dierker, Kim Crumbo, Kelly Smith, Jim Traub, Chris Geanious, Nancy McCloskey, Dick Clark, Martha Clark, Bruce Rumbaugh, Roger Henderson, Joe Biner, and the boys from Illinois. See you downstream.

Dedicated to my parents, Jack and Beverly Coder, my grandparents, George and Mary Ellen McNeal, and Bill and Trudy Coder, who made it possible for me to swim in the stream of culture.

CONTENTS

The well-trained archaeologist working in Grand Canyon, or anywhere else for that matter, must first and foremost be an anthropologist. — Robert C. Euler

PROLOGUE

The Grand Canyon region has been home to humans for more than 13,000 years.

For millions of visitors coming to the canyon each year, the view surpasses even the jaded expectations of modern times. Seeing the place for just a few moments is all it takes to get the canyon in your blood. Usually less than a twenty-four-hour stay, it can be a sine wave of rushing and waiting. Despite the traffic and crowds, the images linger with us. The experience, like salvation, is better felt than told.

To ancient Native Americans the canyon was home, encompassing all of its simple pleasures and complexities: hearth, school, grocery store, church. The evidence in the form of 13,000-year-old spear points, Archaic hunting camps, and worn-down Puebloan villages is spread out across the landscape like weathered veneer, rarely obvious and mostly erased by the relentless processes of time.

Grand Canyon and the region it defines consist of thousands of square miles of incised canyons, mesas, and isolated volcanoes overlain by a spider web of drainages that connected Grand Canyon proper to the world outside and eased the movement of people into and through a region that was otherwise all but inaccessible. Before 1869 no fences or invisible lines crossed the countryside; it just blended into upriver, downriver, and the world beyond the rims. In 1953 Mike Tobin, a Chemehuevi man, when pressed by lawyers of the Indian Claims Commission about the old borders between his people and the Hualapai in his father's time, said simply, "They didn't know nothing about the lines." Lines like that were not a part of their world.

Convolutions, caves, cracks beyond count, and the interstitial space between grains of rock combine to create an unimaginable space within the canyon. Grand Canyon can be measured in length, width, and depth, but its absolute volume cannot be quantified. In the same fashion cultures may be described, but not defined. Some attributes of a culture can be measured, bones scrutinized, pottery and stone tools analyzed, sites mapped to scale, but quantifying the whole is elusive if not impossible. There remains something intangible about the experience that archaeologists, as observers from another age with a different perspective, cannot quite get their arms around.

The notion of time is a human convention designed to track change and motion. People's lives and the cultures they create move through the years as braided streams, leaving ever-changing trails of evidence in their wakes. Some of the evidence clarifies, some of it confuses or begs for more. The goods we create are all subtle indications of the unique behaviors that set us apart from our neighboring cultures in time and in place. Birth and puberty rites, style of burial, style of art, style of warfare, form of worship, food taboos, the games we play (or watch) are all lines on the changing face of culture. As individuals, we are not separated from history merely by the passage of time, but flow with it, connected to the unbroken chain of human events.

Mineral pigments were applied to rock surfaces to create pictograph images. Some are messages, some are counts, and some represent the induced trances of shamans.

A LONG HISTORY

The stream of human history in and around Grand Canyon stretches back at least 13,000 years and probably much longer. Its significance is reflected in the archaeological record and in the oral histories of modern Native Americans. The Hopi consider the canyon and all it contains sacred ground. For them *'ongtupka* is the ances-

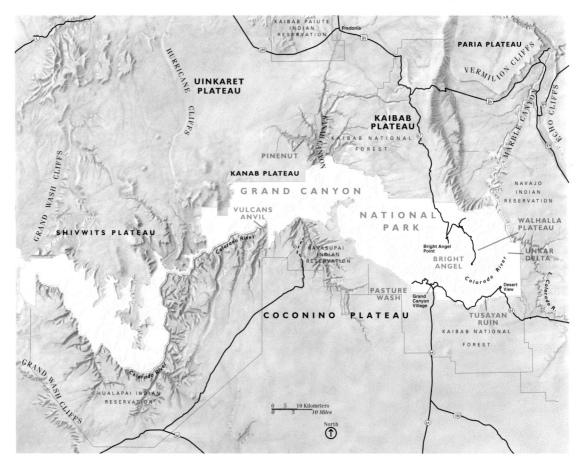

tral home to twenty-three clans that have survived to the present. Other clans at Hopi have other points of origin. The Hopi call Puebloan archaeological sites *kiituvoyla,* house symbols. The remnants of these old Puebloan villages comprise some of the footprints of Hopi clan migrations. Today these footprints serve as cultural markers and remind the Hopi people of their obligations to the land. The trails they established to maintain contact with the canyon hold spiritual meaning, linking modern villages to ancestral lands.

The Hualapai and Havasupai have inhabited the south side of the Colorado River from Desert View westward to Lake Mead for the better part of a millennium. The Havasupai, an old band of the Hualapai Confederation, have been an independent tribe for more than a hundred years, still make their home in the depths of the Grand Canyon system, and consider themselves its guardians.

The Southern Paiute inhabited the north side of the Colorado River for the entire length of Grand Canyon after the Pueblo people left until the mid 1800s. For them it was, and is, *puaxant tuvip,* holy land. Red clan symbols placed on rocks and old camp sites indicate their passing.

A place of Zuni clan origin, *chimik' yana 'kya deya,* is located in the depths of Bright Angel Canyon in the vicinity of Ribbon Falls on the north side of the Colorado River. At some point the people that lived there crossed the river and left the canyon. They moved south to the base of the San Francisco Peaks where they lived for a hundred years or so before they moved on and joined with other people to become the Zuni. The Zuni refer to themselves as the A:shiwi, and call the canyon *ku'nin a' l' akkwe' a.*

The Navajo have been in the region for centuries, but only came into the eastern reaches of the canyon in the last four hundred years or so. The Dil zhc'e', a Western Apache group, ranged as far north as the Grand Canyon to trade, raid, and collect. They appropriately called the expanse *ge da'cho,* edge of the big cliff.

Spanish conquistadors from Coronado's expedition, guided by Hopi men, peered over the south rim in the late summer of 1540. A Jesuit missionary visited the Havasupai in 1776, but before 1869 the canyon was the exclusive domain of the American Indian. The territory, which the United States had obtained from Spain in 1848, was virtually unexplored by European-Americans. To the government in Washington and the captains of manifest destiny, Grand Canyon was a great blank on the map. Several army expeditions skirted the thirty-fifth parallel brushing south of the canyon in the 1850s, hauling wagon loads of gold from California eastward and bringing railroad surveyors and geologists westward. It remained a land of pass-through and saw no settlement by European-Americans until a generation after the Civil War.

'ongtupka
Hopi

gik' mi giv tdé
Hualapai

puaxant tuvip
Southern Paiute

ku'nin a' l' akkwe' a
Zuni

bits' iis ninēēzi
Navajo

ge da'cho
Western Apache

Grand Canyon
Anglo / European

Very little archaeological work was done at Grand Canyon until after 1950. Extensive excavations conducted by Douglas Schwartz on the north rim's Walhalla Plateau and in the river corridor plus more than thirty years of work throughout the canyon by Robert Euler laid the foundation for our current understanding of its cultural history. Numerous park service projects have since fine tuned the basic picture. In 1990–1991 a survey of the river corridor from Glen Canyon Dam to Lake Mead documented more than 475 archaeological sites, tying together the excellent but sporadic earlier work. The river corridor project stretched in excess of 270 miles downstream and illustrates the often overlooked perspective that the canyon is not just a deep hole, it is a long one as well.

Some details of Puebloan life have changed little over the centuries.

Until recently the archaeological focus has been on the Puebloan farmers, popularly known as the Anasazi, and their ancestors from roughly 700 to 1,800 years ago.

John Wesley Powell encountered one of their pueblos at the mouth of Bright Angel Creek during his voyage down the Colorado River in the summer of 1869. Major Powell noted in his journal that he had observed ". . . the ruins of two or three old houses, which were originally of stone laid in mortar. Only the foundations are left, but irregular blocks, of which the houses were constructed, lie scat-

Archaeologists test and map a site in the river corridor.

tered about. In one room I find an old mealing stone, deeply worn, as if it had been much used. A great deal of pottery is strewn around, and the old trails, which in some places are deeply worn into the rocks, are seen."

Bright Angel Pueblo lies less than fifty yards from the river bank, visible at the top of the photo. The pueblo has living areas, a storage structure, and a kiva. In cliffs behind the site, granaries held surplus corn and other dried goods. The room to the upper right of the kiva represents the first occupation of the site, A.D. 1050. The others were built after 1100 and used until about 1140.

N

kiva

room 1

room 2

room 5

room 4

room 3

AN ARCHAEOLOGICAL PERSPECTIVE

Archaeology is defined as the scientific study of past cultures, their material goods (artifacts) and behaviors. Linking a people's everyday possessions to the greater complexity of their culture is tricky. It can be like trying to get at the lives of our great grandparents by deciphering a jar of old buttons and a kerosene lamp. The archaeologist is a cultural detective who must draw upon several disciplines to reconstruct a picture of the past that is as complete as possible. The past becomes more clear with an understanding of landforms (geomorphology), soils, climate, excavation and the laboratory work it generates, such as radiocarbon (C-14) and tree-ring dating, the study of pollen, seeds and fibers, the microscopic wear patterns on tools, and ceramic analysis.

This cache of Puebloan pots, damaged by fallen rock, still holds pieces of the story for archaeologists.

The cultures of Grand Canyon left evidence that is often subtle and not easily interpreted. Time and the elements are pervasive, stripping away the flesh and soft parts without bias. Perishable materials — leather, wood, sinew, plant fiber (baskets), hair — fade quickly with the passage of time. In arid inner-canyon caves and rock shelters, such artifacts are occasionally preserved, but that is the exception and not the rule. Often we must try to decipher a vision of the past based on an assemblage of artifacts that represents the survival of the hardest items — pottery sherds, arrow points, and stone tools — not necessarily the most informative. Petroglyphs and pictographs are additional clues, but the intriguing symbols and abstract images often create more mystery. Ethnographic work with modern tribes adds more critical detail to the story. Today archaeologists rely on Native American expertise for insight into what white culture calls prehistory and what tribal people simply consider history.

Geologists use a concept called facies change to explain the way rock formations undulate across the surface: thick here, thinning in another direction, ultimately disappearing altogether as they become more distant from their source material, eventually merging with other formations emanating from other places. To envision it requires a three-dimensional perspective. The same is true of cultures. They can be hard to trace as they expand and contract, merging with other cultures over time. With time as a factor, studying them becomes a four-dimensional exercise.

In the ongoing tradition of Western Civilization, our scholars have a tendency to divvy up the past into segments, each one of which can be defined by characteristics that set it apart from others: the Paleolithic, the Archaic, the Bronze Age, the Age of Reason, the Roaring Twenties, and so on. For instance, in the American Southwest the Paleolithic period is differentiated from the later Archaic period, to a degree, based on observable changes in projectile-point technologies. The Early Archaic is distinguished

STONE TOOLS

Stone tools are divided into distinct categories: chipped and ground. Chipped stone tools include spear, dart, and arrow points; knife blades; punches; scrapers; awls; gravers; and a variety of other items. They are generally produced from fine-grained or crystalline rock that can be obtained from within the canyon. The Kaibab and Redwall Limestones contain seemingly limitless quantities of workable chert. The cobble bars along the river and benches below the rims hold an enormous supply of knappable rock. Highly valued obsidian and workable rhyolite are common to the immediate region with several sources as close as Flagstaff and Seligman, Arizona.

The metate and mano are used to grind grains into flour. Such groundstone tools are made by pecking and grinding pieces of stone into the desired shape.

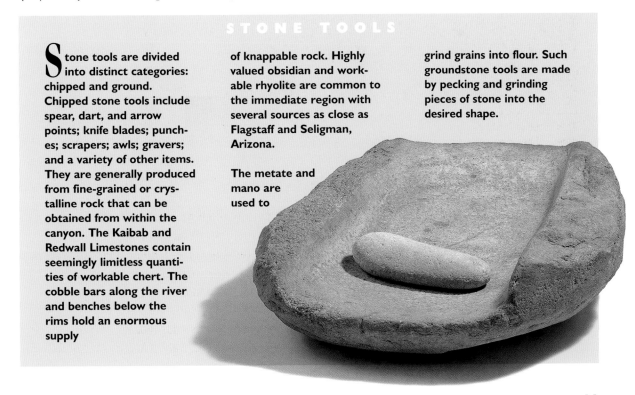

from the Middle Archaic partly based on differing methods of sandal construction and changes in regional climate. Later Puebloan cultures can be distinguished from Archaic sites by the presence of ceramics and the suite of artifacts associated with maize (corn) dependence. But in reality there are few razor-clean breaks in history. Events develop a momentum of their own more complex than can be figured out precisely, with one event influencing the many, and the many the one. As is true of our own lives and the lives of our families, the further we go back in time the more hazy events become. With all that in mind, we can begin to look at the march of human history in Grand Canyon.

Native American elders shed some light on a petroglyph.

Paleo-Indian Hunters

From about 13,000 years ago to more than a million years ago so much of the earth's water was tied up in glacial ice that sea levels were periodically as much as three hundred feet lower than

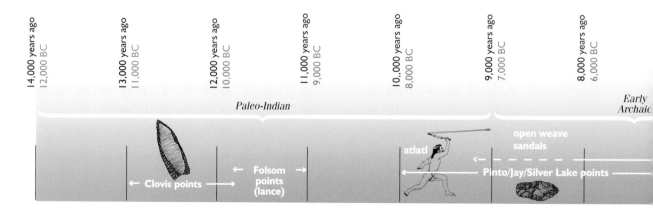

| 14,000 years ago 12,000 BC | 13,000 years ago 11,000 BC | 12,000 years ago 10,000 BC | 11,000 years ago 9,000 BC | 10,,000 years ago 8,000 BC | 9,000 years ago 7,000 BC | 8,000 years ago 6,000 BC |

Paleo-Indian

Early Archaic

← Clovis points →

← Folsom → points (lance)

atlatl

open weave sandals

← Pinto/Jay/Silver Lake points →

today. Long-term cycles of glacial advances and retreats typical during this time regularly exposed a broad shelf of land known as the Bering Land Bridge, which physically connected Siberia and Alaska. As the glaciers grew and water was turned to ice, sea levels dropped and the shelf would appear; as the glaciers melted and the sea rose the shelf would disappear under the waves. Between 40,000 and 13,000 years ago hunters could periodically use this route to migrate from Asia into the interior of Alaska. By 13,000 years ago their tools and rare camps appear in Arizona south of Grand Canyon. Known as the Clovis people, they are named after the town in New Mexico where their meticulously crafted spear points were first discovered with the bones of now-extinct mammoths.

Some archaeologists and many Native Americans reject the Bering Land Bridge as the sole explanation for the populating of the Western Hemisphere. The diversity existing in New World languages, physical make-up of the tribes, and the many complex cultural traditions, such as numerous cultivated crops, it is argued, simply could not have gotten to the point they had by A.D. 1492 from a single source. Polynesian immigration by sea is a given; people coming from southern Asia, less so; but evidence of other mechanisms is scant. Recently excavated sites at the tip of Chile have extended New World human history back more than 20,000 years. It is now accepted by all except the most conservative researchers

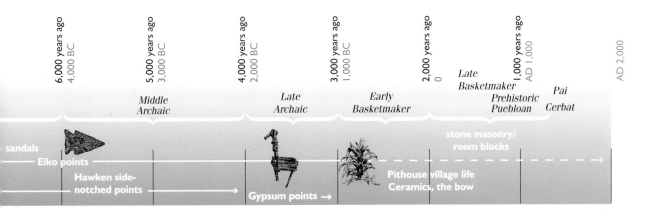

6,000 years ago 4,000 BC	5,000 years ago 3,000 BC	4,000 years ago 2,000 BC	3,000 years ago 1,000 BC	2,000 years ago 0	1,000 years ago AD 1,000	AD 2,000

Middle Archaic

Late Archaic

Early Basketmaker

Late Basketmaker

Prehistoric Puebloan

Pai Cerbat

sandals
Elko points
Hawken side-notched points
Gypsum points →
Pithouse village life
Ceramics, the bow
stone masonry/ room blocks

that humans have been in the New World much longer than previously recognized — in small numbers, perhaps as long ago as 30,000 years.

The Clovis and subsequent Folsom were sophisticated big-game-hunting people. Evidence of their success and passing appears throughout the United States. The Colorado River Basin contains evidence aplenty of the paleohunters. Camps have been found along the San Juan and Green Rivers, as well as on the rocky benches of the Little Colorado River, but at Grand Canyon the traces are confined to a few spear points. They were here, but most of their goods have been ground into dust by the elements, covered over by flood, or scavenged by those who came along later.

Paleo-Indian people were few in number, a small group here, a small group there. They lived life on the go, moving from camp to camp, searching for or following big game. Their possessions were, for the most part, perishable and renewable: leather, bone, wood, and plant fibers. With a mobile hunting people, what is not essential gets left behind and the centuries methodically swallow it up.

It is not known exactly how many people comprised a working band or unit. It no doubt varied — more than a dozen and less than forty, dependent on the available resources and those preferences that are not preserved in the record. Humans are cultural beings and cultures do not exist in a vacuum. Each band was an independent cog in a greater society. These extended-family bands would connect with other related groups at specific times and places to trade goods and stories, reinforce old connections, and

Giant sloths along with camels, mammoths, short-faced bears, and wolves were hunted by the Paleo-Indians of Grand Canyon country.

arrange relationships that transcended the seasons.

The paleohunters of Grand Canyon country were walking the tightrope of changing times. The world was warming up. Analysis of Antarctic ice cores and deep-ocean sediments conducted during the 1990s indicated a radical change in the global climate right around 11,000 years ago. In less than a generation all of the remaining ice was melting. The landscape was rearranging itself accordingly, and the annual cycle of weather was sorting itself into the four distinct seasons we are familiar and comfortable with today. It is from this time that most of the cultures around the world enshrined the memory of the great flood. The Colorado River would have been raging through the canyon for decades, unfordable in any season.

The Colorado Plateau, separating the high country on the north and east from the deserts of the Basin and Range to the west and south, was home to generations of prehistoric people.

Pleistocene megafauna — camels, mammoths, giant sloths, short-faced bears, and wolves — were slowly passing away with the glaciers. The hunters' success at bringing down the largest game helped seal their own fate by hastening the decline of the mammoth herds. As the Pleistocene wound down, so did the spear point size. Small game did not require large points. Late Paleo-Indian points known as Folsom were half the length of the elegant Clovis Tradition blades. The old order was in transition; between 11,000 and 9,000 years ago each successive generation was experiencing the downward spiral of diminishing returns.

Groups of hunters living on the Colorado Plateau changed with their world. The transition was not as difficult as it would first seem. Paleo-Indian people had been skimming the big calories but there was still plenty to eat. They fine tuned their hunting strategies to acquire deer, bighorn sheep, and smaller, quicker animals. Hunting deer might not have been as dangerous as taking down mammoths; however, it would by caloric necessity have to occur more often. It also took less cooperation, which would change to some degree the ties that bound individuals and families.

This broken Folsom blade from Grand Canyon is tantalizing evidence that Paleo-Indian hunters were moving through the Nankoweap Basin more than 10,000 years ago.

Changes in tactics are signified by changes in the tool kit and this is accordingly manifested in the archaeological record. In the Archaic Period that was to follow, the hand-held spear hafted with large, fluted blades was replaced by the atlatl (a spear-thrower) and shorter, lighter darts tipped with smaller projectile points. Plants became a more critical source of food. Groundstone hand tools and grinding surfaces required to process seeds, nuts, and other materials appear more often in the record after the demise of the large Ice Age game. The patterns of regional movement changed and the mobile hunters began to establish home territories rather than simply following the herds.

Folsom, Humboldt, Jay, Mohave Lake, and Pinto style blades and projectile points belonging to Late Paleo-Indian and Early Archaic stone tool traditions are found across the uplands of Grand Canyon National Park. This indicates that small groups of people remained in the region even as the big game died out. Their low population and light hand on the landscape did not generate enough material to be easily recognized or discovered.

DIMINISHING RETURNS

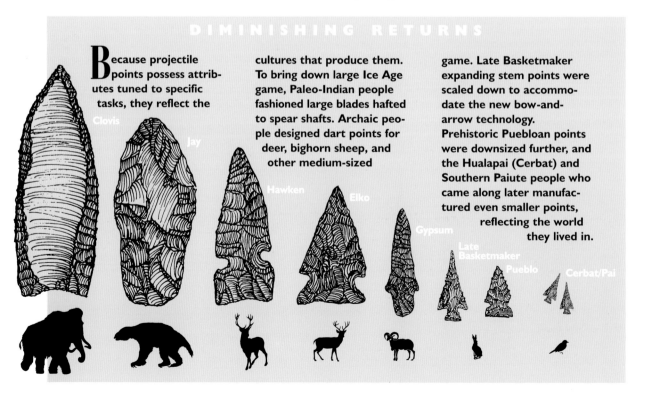

Because projectile points possess attributes tuned to specific tasks, they reflect the cultures that produce them. To bring down large Ice Age game, Paleo-Indian people fashioned large blades hafted to spear shafts. Archaic people designed dart points for deer, bighorn sheep, and other medium-sized game. Late Basketmaker expanding stem points were scaled down to accommodate the new bow-and-arrow technology. Prehistoric Puebloan points were downsized further, and the Hualapai (Cerbat) and Southern Paiute people who came along later manufactured even smaller points, reflecting the world they lived in.

The Archaic Period

By 9,000 years ago, more people had entered the Grand Canyon region from the Basin and Range Province to the northwest with all the trappings of Archaic culture: atlatl and darts, open-weave sandals, seasonal habitations, groundstone tools. Indication of human settlement in Grand Canyon country during the long centuries of the Archaic is extensive. The Archaic period in the American Southwest is such an expanse of human history that it has been divided into three parts: Early, Middle, and Late. These broad divisions are based on several factors: changes in projectile point technology, alterations in climate, and regional shifts in population.

Early Archaic culture is transitional from paleoculture reflecting the loss of the large Pleistocene game animals and a drier climate. Despite these seemingly major inconveniences, the human population on the plateau increased during this period. People slowed down a notch. The pace of life and drier climate were more conducive to preserving what the human experience chose to offer up. So the record from these times is more complete and a little less mysterious than the Paleo-Indian. About 6,500 years ago the climate became drier still, signaling the beginning of the Middle-Archaic drought that would last off and on for almost 2,000 years.

As the West dried up, erosion accelerated. With each generation there was less plant cover holding the softer sediment in place. Sand was released into the system in large quantities. The larger rivers became sluggish and smaller rivers clogged up. The reliable springs turned into seeps and the seeps disappeared completely. Gullies dissected the dry landscape. Old terrace systems were etched back and removed. The wind gathered sand into dunes and choked every empty space.

The introduction of the atlatl (a spear-thrower) greatly improved the odds for the Archaic hunter.

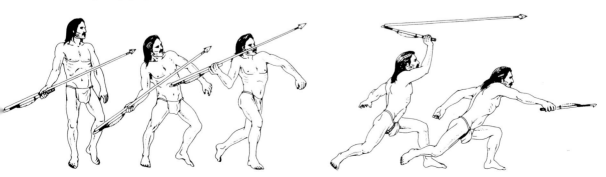

Over the period of a person's lifetime the environment went through a perceptible change. Over three lifetimes it changed dramatically. People would have to go five times as far to get half as much. At some point people say enough is enough. One option would be to leave the region and take their chances on the road. The other would be to tough it out. For those choosing to stay, the large rock shelters were a poor option and were mostly abandoned. As the springs associated with the shelters failed, people were forced to relocate to the dwindling sources of permanent water. The groups that had remained to weather it out with the landscape refocused their efforts on the shriveling resource base with which they were confronted.

Stantons Cave

The few people still moving between the canyons and plateaus would occasionally camp on the soft sand that sifted into caves that had been inhabited throughout the Early Archaic. They would repair their goods, build fires, rest, and move on, leaving on the surface traces of their passing, some of which would be incorporated into the record of the cave.

The highly erosive nature of the Grand Canyon system constantly reworks the sedimentary deposits. Soils older than 5,000 years are rare. Nevertheless, Middle Archaic sites have been recorded in a tributary of Glen Canyon. Bowns Canyon, located upstream from Lees Ferry, harbored a community that endured the hard times by taking up residence in a place with a permanent source of good water.

By 4,500 years ago the severe dry times were waning and populations were flowing back. There is a good deal of Late Archaic evidence found at Grand Canyon. The Gypsum points these people used are commonly found in the park north of the river. One of the best examples of Archaic culture is the elaborate pictograph panel known as Shamans Gallery located on the north rim.

Perched fifty feet above the river in a narrow stretch of Marble Canyon is a large opening in the Redwall Limestone. Stantons Cave reveals a story of Late Archaic hunters who came and went in this remote spot more than 4,000 years ago. Excavations in the cave uncovered dozens of split-willow-branch figurines. Many are run through by small twigs representing spears.

An artist's view of the Archaic people's hunting-and-gathering lifeway.

They are the shadows of human behavior. More recently, hikers have found figurines in the Nankoweap Basin, and they are found across the Great Basin into Nevada, telling us these particular people were part of a larger ranging culture.

The Late Archaic people of Grand Canyon acquired life's necessities from the stacked resources between the river and rim country. They hunted bighorn sheep in the gorge, scoured side canyons for mineral pigments and medicinal plants, harvested pinyon nuts, and hunted deer in the uplands. They had dogs, wore adornment, traded for goods outside the region, made fire, wore buckskin clothes. They did not make or use pottery. They made baskets. They pondered their existence. Their skeletons are very rare. Not much else about them is known. Like the paleohunters before them, their goods were mostly perishable. So we are — again — faced with defining an entire people by a few tools, some figurines, and an occasional thought-provoking pictograph panel.

They lived quietly on a landscape they were intimate with, not necessarily without conflict, but without a lot of noise just the same. They possessed an understanding of

Figurines, made by shaping and wrapping two halves of a split willow twig into the likeness of a deer or bighorn sheep, are found across Nevada, parts of Utah, and in Grand Canyon north of the Colorado River. Strikingly similar to images seen in Archaic petroglyphs, they are diagnostic of Late Archaic culture. Usually found in dry caves, the figurines are of varying dimensions, but most are palm-sized. They may have been charms used in pre-hunting rituals.

Rock art refers to the various designs and symbols placed on a rock surface

Puebloan petroglyph

by the human hand. Some individuals take exception to the term. The form is artistic, but to the Native American calling it art is misleading at best and at worst offensive.

Two major categories are recognized: (1) Petroglyphs are pecked or scratched into the rock face creating a negative surface and revealing the lighter rock underneath; (2) Pictographs are created by applying pigment to the rock, leaving a positive color image on the surface. The most common colors are black (charcoal), red

(hematite), white (kaolinite), yellow (limonite), blue and green (oxides of copper).

Rock inscriptions are not language, and the meanings are as diverse as human behavior. Some are the enigmatic visions of a shaman

Pigments

emerging from an extended trance, some are clan symbols signifying use or a claim, some are stories, some are directions, and others that appear to be only smudges or colored streaks are the prayers of individual men and women.

Detail of Shamans Gallery pictograph.

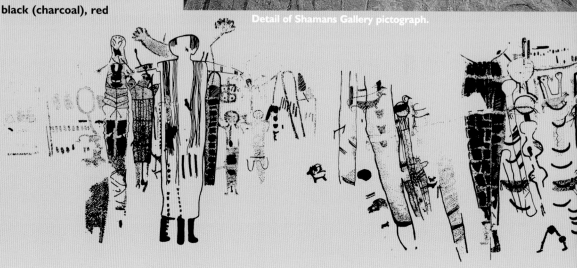

Glyphs and graphs act as cultural and individual signatures, adding color and flesh

Puebloan petroglyphs

to the archaeological skeleton of old walls, sherds, and chipped stone. On occasion styles can be connected to a specific language group or cultural tradition and with some success can be dated.

Hopi clan symbols

Fremont pictograph

Hopi clan symbols are present at the Salt Cave, and an unusual petroglyph placed on a bedrock bench below Lees Ferry is associated with the *Newe:Kwe* (Galaxy Fraternity) of the Zuni. A pictograph panel in the west end of the canyon commemorates the Paiute Ghost Dance of the late 1800s. Old Puebloan and Late Archaic panels are found throughout the canyon region.

The preservation and protection of these prehistoric records is vital, as their significance to the archaeological record is still being unraveled.

Puebloan petroglyph

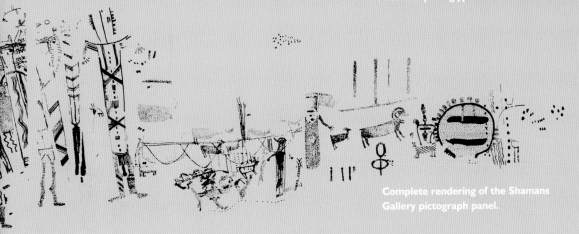
Complete rendering of the Shamans Gallery pictograph panel.

plants and animals, water and rock, climate and season that is really beyond our grasp. Theirs was not a scientific perspective, but one of intuition and experience accumulated by trial and error for literally millennia. Knowledge was passed generation-to-generation by imitation and the spoken word when life, education, and culture were synonymous.

The Basketmakers

The earliest corn-growing people at Grand Canyon are commonly known as the Basketmaker culture. They cultivated corn, but still hunted game and gathered wild plant foods. These people were scattered around Grand Canyon in family camps and small villages. There is botanical evidence from samples collected at Nankoweap

CORN: A CHANGE IN THE WIND

During the Late Archaic the opportunity for groups of hunters to scale down the degree of mobility in their lives was at hand. Corn (maize), beans, and squash have been under cultivation in the Valley of Mexico for at least 9,000 years. But it was not until 3,500 years ago that people moving northward out of the Mexican highlands brought corn into the American Southwest. By 3,000 years ago it was being grown locally on the Colorado Plateau south of the Colorado River. By 2,500 years ago it had jumped the Grand Canyon onto the Arizona Strip and northward into Utah. Corn changed everything.

Alterations to a pattern of life established over centuries, like stopping to plant corn, are not made casually, and it is not something that happens overnight. The repercussions are numerous. Nutrition, social fabric, spiritual focus, and the routine of numerous daily tasks must change to accommodate the new order that comes with village life and dependence on maize. People must ease their way into it. For some these changes were not acceptable and not all of the groups living in northern Arizona chose the road that led to small-scale farming.

Historically, some Western Apache and Navajo families grew corn, others did not. The choice was based on personal preference, and that may be a clue to how certain people eased into this way of life at Grand Canyon.

Delta that they were growing cotton in the river corridor 1,300 years ago. They lived in rock shelters where available and otherwise in pithouses, underground homes that were entered through a hole in the roof. Pithouses were well insulated, being cool in the summer and warm in the winter.

By 1,100 years ago most of the farmers had traded the pit-house for the above-ground stone roomblock. In the centuries to come, some of the Basketmaker groups that would become known as the Anasazi retained the pithouse design as the ceremonial kiva.

An artist's view of a Basketmaker community with pithouses.

Items that set the Basketmakers apart from other cultures were cradleboards with soft headrests, squaretoed sandals, beautiful woven bags, subterranean slab-lined storage cists, intricate baskets, and curved throwing sticks for hunting small game. They wove with such skill that their baskets were watertight. In fact, they cooked by adding heated rocks to concoctions of water and foodstuffs contained in such a vessel. Seeds and nuts were parched by flipping them in a tray with small, hot stones.

They did not begin to make pottery until about 1,700 years ago. About that same time, the bow and arrow were replacing the atlatl and dart. It is likely the bow was brought into the Southwest by Shoshone-speaking hunters from the Columbia Plateau. This masterful innovation further downsized projectile points. The bow

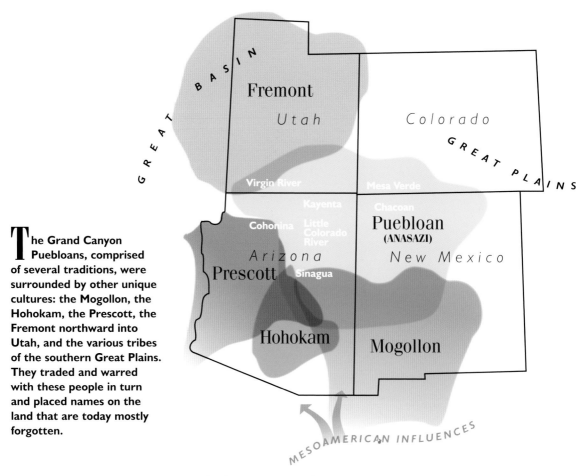

The Grand Canyon Puebloans, comprised of several traditions, were surrounded by other unique cultures: the Mogollon, the Hohokam, the Prescott, the Fremont northward into Utah, and the various tribes of the southern Great Plains. They traded and warred with these people in turn and placed names on the land that are today mostly forgotten.

made the acquisition of game an even less communal affair by making the individual hunter more effective. It also would have changed the tactics of raiding and local warfare. A good archer with a big jar of water and a family for motivation would have been difficult to dislodge. It took more than two centuries for this new technology to jump the Colorado River and move southward off the Colorado Plateau into the low deserts.

The Puebloans

By 1,250 years ago what is today recognized as Basketmaker culture was all but replaced by the lifestyle of the pueblo. Like the evolution of the thirteen original European colonies into the European-American United States, it was a process, not an event. Remembering the facies change concept used by geologists, we can say Basketmaker culture grades into Pueblo culture.

Anasazi is the popular term used to describe various maize-dependent prehistoric Puebloan cultures inhabiting the southern portions of the Colorado Plateau and the Four Corners regions from Late Basketmaker times until about seven hundred years ago. Anasazi is derived from two Navajo words meaning enemy ancestor, ancient enemy, or words to that effect. Something is lost in translation, but it does illustrate the potentially hostile relationship that can exist between the semi-nomadic hunter and the villager.

The prehistoric Puebloans were not a homogenous people. Archaeologists have differentiated them roughly into eastern and western divisions and further into several traditions based on location, social organization, ceramic styles, and architecture. The traditions are Chacoan, Mesa Verde, Kayenta, Virgin River, Little Colorado River, Cohonina, and to a lesser degree, the Sinagua. At Grand Canyon the Kayenta and Virgin traditions blend and merge on the north side of the Colorado River, just as the Kayenta and Cohonina intermingle in time and space on the south side. The various western branches probably spoke different tongues of a broader language family believed to have been Uto-Aztecan. It was common historically for American Indians to speak multiple languages. This was assuredly the case a thousand years ago amongst a trading people like the prehistoric Pueblo and their neighbors.

These distinct groups were aligned by trade, maize dependence, material culture, and possibly by religion. The relationships between and within Puebloan centers changed over time and oscillated from amicable alliances and interdependent trading to raiding and dominance through religious and economic control, the likes of which spread outward from and retreated to Chaco Canyon.

Prior to a thousand years ago isolated settlements of Puebloans lived in the uplands along the rims and farmed in the

ARCHAEOLOGICAL DIVISIONS

Archaeologists in the early twentieth century divided the prehistoric Pueblo into temporal divisions based on advances in architecture, land-use patterns, and design styles found on pottery. These divisions serve as a framework for studying the past, but would be meaningless if presented to a farmer in Grand Canyon a thousand years ago. The designations of Basketmaker II, III and Pueblo I, II, III relegate an entire culture to stylistic changes in material goods and do not address the more difficult task of understanding economics, migration, social fabric, and religion.

An·a·sa´·zi

Anasazi is a term derived from two **Navajo** words meaning enemy ancestor or ancient enemy. To the **Hopi** and **Zuni**, "enemy ancestor" is a politically charged idea not acceptable as a name for their relatives. The **Hopi** prefer *Hisatsinom,* ancient ancestors or old ones, to signify this early connection. Be that as it may, Anasazi has a ring to it. The term has come into standard use by scholars, and captured the public's imagination. In this text prehistoric Puebloan is used.

25

Thick-plaited yucca fiber tells us the sandal above is prehistoric Puebloan. Sandals, like the one at the right, of the older Basketmaker culture were more painstakingly made.

river corridor, tending small plots of corn, squash, and cotton as conditions would allow. In 1991 a flash flood in Chuar Canyon uncovered a classic assemblage of pottery sherds in a cutbank dating to the Pueblo I period, nearly 1,200 years ago, revealing the presence of a productive farming community that existed along the river 200 years before the Puebloan renaissance at Grand Canyon.

Around 1,000 years ago the climate began to shift once again, this time to the advantage of farmers. A slight increase in the amount of seasonal precipitation allowed corn, beans, squash, and cotton to be grown with reliability in more places. This change in the rain belt temporarily allowed Kayenta farmers to expand across the Colorado Plateau wherever a crop could be coaxed from the soil. This included the San Juan River country in Utah, the Kaibito Plateau, and downstream along the Colorado River through Glen Canyon into Grand Canyon. It also allowed the Cohonina already established along the south rim to expand and flourish. Chaco Canyon, to the east, rose to dominance at about the same time.

Successful farmers, traders, and craftsmen, the Puebloans were calculated opportunists. Farmers are conservative by nature, and risk takers by necessity, balancing what they can grow with the quality of soil and the availability of water. A slight miscalculation, and the very young and the old die. Two bad years in a row and the strongest are staring at an empty plate. Farmers are always thinking ahead and taking advantage of subtle changes in the environment. This is what happened at Grand Canyon. Farmers recognized an opportunity and expanded into the canyon like water pouring into a dry stream channel. Carrying their infants, bows, water jugs and seed, small children and dogs in tow, they moved westward from their old homes. Within a generation they had occupied virtually every delta and quarter-acre of arable ground in Grand Canyon.

Corn was the bulwark of Puebloan life, being central not only to the table, but to the daily fabric of the community. However, a steady diet of corn can lead to a variety of ailments stemming from a lack of B-complex vitamins and certain amino acids. The high starch content forms sugars that wreak havoc in the mouth, causing tooth decay and painful, life-threatening abscesses not seen in groups where wild foods dominate the diet. This serious problem can be alleviated by soaking corn in ashes (which contain lye) to turn it into vitamin-B-rich hominy. If corn is complemented with squash and beans, major nutritional problems can be averted. This New World triad of corn, beans, and squash provides the carbohydrates, protein, amino acids, and vitamin A that the body needs. If the spice of life — chilies — are available, then vitamin C is added to the equation.

But the people could not afford to be just farmers. The climate at Grand Canyon would not allow it. Even with broad alluvial terraces, increased precipitation, and a higher water table, which are all gone today, farming was still risky business. So in addition to farming they capitalized on the natural resources available to them. When the menu can be supplemented by wild plants and animals, everybody is that much better off. Prickly-pear fruit and rose hips are rich in vitamin C, pinyon nuts are high in good fat and protein. Because of their broad resource base, Puebloans living at Grand Canyon were probably a healthier group of people than their urban cousins in Chaco Canyon. Useful things were stacked one on top of the other for a vertical mile, from the river to the rim. There were in this vast

COHONINA CULTURE

The Cohonina people who inhabited the Coconino Plateau during Puebloan times were a Basketmaker-tradition people who had moved from the north side of the canyon to south of the river prior to 1,300 years ago. The Cohonina maintained a presence along the south rim and down in the canyon west of Desert View, regularly trading with their contemporary Kayenta neighbors south of the river and less so with the Virgin branch on the north rim. A diffuse Cohonina community of small settlements and single-family farmsteads in the area of Pasture Wash west of today's Grand Canyon Village on the south rim intermingles with sites that are purely Kayenta. Artifacts produced by both cultures are found on both types of sites — Cohonina arrow points on Kayenta sites and Kayenta pottery on Cohonina sites. Apparently there was a period 900 to 1,000 years ago when relations between the two overlapping groups were amiable and advantageous to both. By 850 years ago whatever had kept them at Grand Canyon had run out. By A.D. 1150 they were gone. Those remaining at the canyon would be absorbed by the Hualapai moving eastward out of the Mojave Desert.

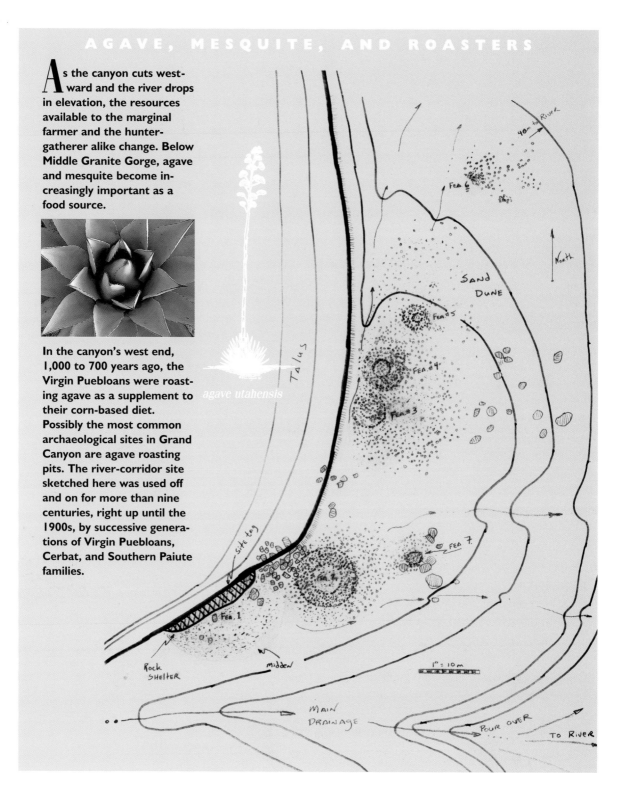

As the canyon cuts west-ward and the river drops in elevation, the resources available to the marginal farmer and the hunter-gatherer alike change. Below Middle Granite Gorge, agave and mesquite become increasingly important as a food source.

In the canyon's west end, 1,000 to 700 years ago, the Virgin Puebloans were roasting agave as a supplement to their corn-based diet. Possibly the most common archaeological sites in Grand Canyon are agave roasting pits. The river-corridor site sketched here was used off and on for more than nine centuries, right up until the 1900s, by successive generations of Virgin Puebloans, Cerbat, and Southern Paiute families.

agave utahensis

Talus

40m to River

Fea 6

North

Sand Dune

Fea 5

Fea 4

Fea 3

site tag

Fea 7

Fea 2

Fea 1

midden

Rock Shelter

1" : 10 m

MAIN DRAINAGE

POUR OVER

TO RIVER

arid country edible cactus, mesquite beans, yucca, agave (mescal), grass seeds, acorns, walnut and pinyon nuts, wild fruit, greens and herbs, and plants used as medicines, dyes, and for ceremony. Yucca had multiple uses: the fruit for food, fibers for cordage, and the root for soap as well as pliable red strands used in basket design. Animals utilized included bighorn sheep, deer, bear, bobcat, mountain lion, rock squirrel, mice, packrats, woodrats, eagles and hawks, waterfowl, chuckwalla, and small lizards. Like the later Hualapai, the farmers were apparently, by choice, not fishermen.

There were raw materials in abundance: wood for fuel, chert from the Kaibab and Redwall Limestones, cobbles for hammer stones, a dozen textures of sandstone for manos and metates, valuable mineral pigments, serpentine for jewelry, good clean salt precipitating out of the 575-million-year-old Tapeats Sandstone, soil, and, most important of all, water.

The Delta Puebloans

In the eastern Grand Canyon there is a series of large side canyons that drain into the Colorado River. These tributaries breech the incredibly rugged terrain existing between the forested rims and the seemingly desolate inner canyon. Acting as the routes of daily life, the side canyons were the highways by which the inhabitants accessed the stair-step ecology of Grand Canyon.

Each of these side-canyon systems creates a large delta at river level suitable for farming. The deltas focused settlement. The big canyons, Nankoweap, Kwagunt, and Unkar, drain into the Colorado from the north, the Palisades-Tanner-Cardenas systems from the south. Several secondary side canyons such as South Canyon, Basalt Canyon, Sixty-Mile Canyon, Chuar Canyon, and Fossil Creek had small workable deltas occupied by the prehistoric Pueblo. In those days an extensive system of alluvial terraces also existed in the river corridor adding considerable ground that could be cultivated.

The delta farmers of Grand Canyon were double cropping, farming both the inner canyon and the rims while taking advantage of naturally occurring calories throughout the system. They stored food to use as needed through the winter. Below the rims in the lower elevations of the canyon's western reaches, agave (mescal)

The momentous eleventh century — across the world and within the region, this century was a time of change. The Hohokam, Fremont, and Mogollon cultures were flourishing. The multiple eruptions of Sunset Crater, outside of Flagstaff, in the 1060s instigated the earliest wave of Sinagua settlements in the area where Wupatki would be built eighty years later. On the southern Great Plains, Native Americans were moving into villages and growing corn. In Scotland, Macbeth was slain by Duncan in 1050. In 1066 the Normans invaded England and were on the offensive throughout Europe. It was the Fugiwara Epoch in Japan and the beginning of the cult of the Samurai. The Toltecs ruled central Mexico. Cahokia, along the banks of the Mississippi River in what is today Illinois, was the largest city in North America.

was available in the early spring, greens would be popping up along the river, and by April people could gather a variety of edible plants. As soon as the time was deemed proper, corn, beans, squash, and cotton were planted along the river. On the rims, crops planted in late spring matured through the early fall and the upland harvest would dovetail nicely with the ripening pinyon nuts and the best months for deer hunting.

The strategy adopted by the delta farmers in the pursuit of an adequate diet is best illustrated by the geographic relationship between Unkar Delta, elevation 2,600 feet above sea level, and Walhalla Glades on the north rim, 7,800 feet in elevation. Unkar Canyon, which connects the two, allows access to the often snow-covered pine forest of the Walhalla Plateau from the delta at Unkar in just a few hours on foot.

The Walhalla Plateau can get more than two hundred inches of snow a year. Because of the high elevation, snow can still be present on the ground in May. The moisture derived as the late snow pack melts is held by the soil and allows the seeds planted in late spring to germinate. The porous and highly fractured Kaibab Limestone that caps the canyon rims as a rule does not permit water to stand on the surface so there are no ponds, small streams, or springs to rely on. Any moisture from the late snow the fragile soils can retain is critical to the survival of a rim crop until the monsoonal rains come in July or August. The large, locally made ceramic vessels known as ollas, some of which will hold about twenty gallons, could be packed with snow and kept in the shade for watering the young plants in

Unkar Delta on the Colorado River is visible from Walhalla Plateau. The difference in elevation from point to point is about 5,200 feet.

the critical time prior to the coming of the monsoon. The farmers also scraped shallow cisterns into the limestone and lined them with clay in order to pool crucial water. But the presence of adequate soil and a sustainable supply of water were still not enough to guarantee a crop on the north rim.

Temperature is the third factor critical to growing corn and it seems unlikely that Walhalla was warm enough long enough. What really allowed for this high and windy spot to yield a crop was the unique circumstance of the spot itself. Enter the grand design of Mother Nature. The Puebloan sites at Walhalla Glades are perched on the edge of an abyss. During late spring and early fall, when most locations in the surrounding countryside can experience a sudden killer frost, the glades are bathed through the night and on into early morning by great drafts of warm air ascending the vertical walls of the canyon, surging over the rim onto the gardens. Corn and vine crops do best when allowed to mature in conditions where nighttime temperatures exceed fifty degrees Fahrenheit. This warm air convection allowed the natural sugars within the plants to set, causing larger and tastier yields.

Among its many ecological complexities, the Grand Canyon is also a massive breathing device. Just as the canyon walls direct the warm air upward, the intricate web of drainages and side canyons funnel cold air down into the main canyon through the late night and early morning hours. Nightly temperatures can vary as much as twelve degrees between a slope and its companion drainage only a hundred yards away. For fear of killing frosts, most habitation and agricultural sites on the north rim are not found in valley bottoms where the chilled air settles and where soils might be richer, but on the gentler slopes closer to the rapture-inducing cliffs.

Large ollas, such as this corregated vessel fitted with a fiber lattice for carrying, could hold as much as twenty gallons of water.

The gardens at Walhalla Glades would have been busy places from late spring through fall hunting season, but the over two hundred inches of snow per year would have made winter habitation miserable. Chances are good that nobody wintered over, especially in view of the fact that the sunny desert was a few hours walk downslope and travel to the south and the lower elevations to the west would have been practical. This makes even more sense when taking into consideration the winter river would have been low and more easily crossed. Snow is uncommon at river level, but the temperature can and does fall below freezing regularly. During the archaeological survey of 1990–1991 the rafts would occasionally freeze to the clay on the beachs.

Most of the delta farmers would have been found along the river corridor and in the bench country below the rim after the first snows through spring planting. After an early spring planting on the deltas and terraces of the inner canyon, families farming the rims would have moved upward as the snows melted, prepping their plots, upgrading terraces and check dams, making sure the clay-lined reservoirs and ollas were full, getting everything ready for planting.

Remnants of seasonal dwellings and walled gardens are found on the Walhalla Plateau. It is unlikely anyone wintered over during Puebloan times.

Conversely, the inner canyon is very hot May through September, so any reason to be on the rims during summer would have been sufficient. Despite the heat someone was needed to tend the crops along the river during the summer: watering the maturing plants, keeping the ravens at bay, and praying for early rain.

Effort was focused on the planting, maintenance, harvesting, and storing of crops. This was not only a physical effort, but a spiritual and religious exercise requiring cooperation. Life was not partitioned into work, home, church, and lessons. It was one package.

Individuals as well as families considered themselves extensions of the local community, not separate from it. The clan relationships which perpetuate order and enforce the unwritten social regulations in small close-knit communities are extensive and complex and include selecting the proper marriage partner, food taboos, who your cousins are, hunting prohibitions and so on. Farmers may or may not be more devout than one group or another, but they do tend to be meticulous about tradition and usually incorporate devotion into the ritual of daily life, including caring for the growing corn.

GRAND CANYON THERMALS

Anyone who has spent time in the river corridor or camped on the edge of the canyon has experienced the exchange of warm air with cold and vice versa. It may be good for high-altitude farming, but it makes wintertime river trips just that much more uncomfortable. Here is what happens: Most people start getting up around six a.m. It is pitch black. Most of your gear is damp. Within the hour the pale light comes. You cannot see the sun, but it is drawing heat upward, and cold air is being sucked down from the high country, channeled through the side canyons to the river, spewing a tide of frozen air out across the deltas. Within minutes, the temperature drops eight, ten, sometimes fourteen degrees. So you wait for the direct sunlight to come, which can be two or three hours away.

The survival of Puebloan farmers depended on understanding this phenomenon. Knowing where crops were harmed and where they would benefit from the convection was critical. For the modern river runner or archaeologist it might mean the inconvenience of cold feet, but for the canyon's inhabitants 900 years ago it was the difference between a bumper crop and starvation.

In farming communities people do what is required in accordance with the rhythm of tradition and in response to the dramatic events beyond human control: unusually big floods, rainless monsoons, raiding parties with better weapons, bumper crops of insects. Tactics used by the farming settlements throughout Grand Canyon were fine tuned to their particular home bases. The Kayenta and Cohonina villages around Pasture Wash, the isolated Virgin Pueblo at Pinenut on the Kaibab Plateau, the several families at Tapeats and Deer Creek Falls, those in the vicinity of South Canyon, and the delta farmers would have had schedules specific to their own needs.

As the weather allowed, individuals and groups spread out within their resource zones as necessitated by the demands of the season. Life required simultaneous attention to several tasks in sev-

Ceramics are crucial in confirming dates for habitation sites. Archaeologists classify ceramics based on clay type, temper, color, technique of manufacture (coil and scrape, paddle and anvil), paint (mineral or carbon), and surface design. Once classified as a recognized "ware," vessels are further assigned to types and styles. For example, Tusayan White Ware, a Kayenta Puebloan type found in Grand Canyon, evolved over time into various styles of painted design.

Often wares have unique attributes. Crushed olivine temper from volcanic rock makes broken sherds of Virgin Moapa Ware seem to be filled with tiny emeralds. Manganese-rich clays from the canyons east of Kanab, Utah, give Shinarump Wares a distinctive purple cast.

Ceramic types have variable duration in the archaeological record. For instance, Black Mesa Black-on-White was produced without notable change for 300 years. On the other hand, a type of Tsegi Orange Ware known as Medicine Black-on-Red was made for only about 50 years.

We largely define the prehistoric Pueblo by their pottery. Beautiful black-on-red, black-on-white, polychrome, and plainware vessels were produced, traded, and used on a large scale for several centuries. Formal decorated wares were highly valued and extensively traded, while corrugated plainware was made in each community for everday use in storage and food preparation. Sometimes whole vessels were buried with individuals.

People repaired cracked vessels by drilling small holes on each side of the crack and stitching it with yucca or hair cordage. They recycled sherds of broken pots by grinding them smooth and shaping them into pendants, spoons, scraping tools for wet pottery, and spindle whorls for cotton yarn. They used sherds to chink walls of the pueblo and ground them up as temper for new pots.

Tusayan White Ware, like clothing fashion or car designs, evolved over time, into various styles of black painted design. Identifying these can help frame a specific site into a window of time.

Kana-a – A.D. 725-950

Black Mesa – A.D. 875-1150

Sosi – A.D. 1050-1200

Dogoszhi – A.D. 1075-1200

Flagstaff – A.D. 1100-1275

eral places throughout the year: tending crops, watching small children, processing corn, hunting, making new pots and fixing old ones, gathering materials for baskets, collecting medicine, repairing granaries, feeding the turkeys, visiting, haggling with traders, keeping the faith, and keeping watch. Everyone had a job to do. Nothing was wasted.

LANGUAGE FAMILY	LANGUAGE GROUP	LANGUAGE/PEOPLE
Nadene	Athapaskan	Navajo/Apache
Uto-Aztecan	Numic	Southern Paiute
Uto-Aztecan	Hopic	Hopi
Hokan	Yuman	Hualapai/Yavapai
Zuni	Zuni	Zuni
Kiowa-Tanoan	Tiwa	Taos
Indo-European	Romance	French/Italian
Indo-European	Germanic	English/Dutch

Languages change at predictable rates over time, allowing linguists to determine when certain groups of people diverged from each other. Like countries and buildings, languages accommodate widely varying numbers of people. Nadene, for instance, includes hundreds of thousands of Navajo and other Apache speakers. Only about a thousand people fluently speak Zuni, which is its own exclusive language family.

LIFE EXPECTANCY

Accepted data for prehistoric Puebloan longevity from old studies indicates average life spans of twenty-nine to forty years. This age is artificially low, brought down by infant mortality and high death rates for children less than seven years old. In fact, a singular lack of infectious diseases in the New World prior to European contact would, barring starvation and trauma, tend to make for an overall healthy native population. However, studies tell of a hard life for Pueblo people: lower leg breaks associated with desert farming, episodes of severe malnutrition, debilitating arthritis, teeth often worn down to the gum line, abscesses, and the maladies of hard work.

A PROFILE OF PUEBLOAN LIFE

Tusayan Pueblo as it may have appeared around A.D. 1185.

Rock is the essence of Grand Canyon, and rock dominated the lives of its ancient human populations. They lived on, in, and around rock; they sheltered themselves with it, cached critical food stores in it, and with it tried to hedge against erosion, the canyon's moving force. Despite the inherent difficulties, for centuries ancient Puebloan culture flourished on stony ingredients.

Architecture

The Puebloans built a wide array of permanent stone structures, roofed with wood beams, crosshatched by branches and sealed with clay, as well as expedient seasonal ramadas and shelters of posts and brush. A variety of configurations exist throughout Grand Canyon: linear blocks of rectangular rooms, D-shaped and bow-shaped pueblos with attached plazas, L-shaped configurations with wind breaks, detached circular rooms, stone partitions placed in overhangs. This variation reflected personal preference, local conditions, available materials, even clan affiliation and illustrates at a very essential level that Puebloan civilization was anything but homogenous. These people spent most of their lives outside, going indoors because of bad weather or for a specific activity. The prehistoric Puebloan idea of personal space would differ from a modern western one. No one had their own bedroom. There was one bathroom, outside. At any rate, finding personal space likely was not a problem at Grand Canyon. Anyone who required private time would have had their own select places to go to without the necessity of retiring to a small, poorly lit room.

The wide variety of room-block configurations found at Grand Canyon indicate the eclectic nature of western Puebloan construction design and a level of creative and practical expression that is also reflected in their ceramic production.

A farmer's worries are never put to rest. The harvest must be secured and protected, not only from those who might come and take it, but from the enemies living amongst the people themselves: rodents, insects, moisture, and sunlight. Corn, squash, beans, prickly pear fruit, meat, and pinyon nuts would be processed and stored for winter.

After the families' needs were covered, sufficient seed was counted out for the next planting and any surplus was prudently set aside for trade, social events, and that bad year always looming on the horizon. Within a pueblo the majority of structural space was generally devoted to storage. At the Pinenut site, an isolated Virgin farmstead west of Kanab Canyon on the north rim, a living room accommodating the entire family was attached to a linear string of smaller rooms. Here 70 percent of the square footage was devoted to storage space. More than 75 percent of the 2,000 pottery sherds recovered from this site were from broken storage jars.

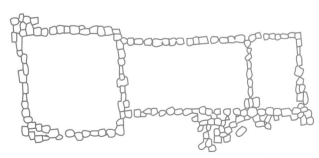

Cliff-face granaries in Clear Creek Canyon.

After the home capacity was used up, people built clusters and individual granaries in the cliffs. They found a suitable location, walled it up with stone and clay, then meticulously fitted it with a

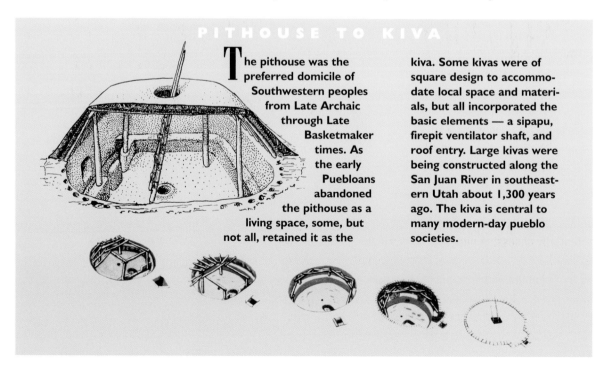

PITHOUSE TO KIVA

The pithouse was the preferred domicile of Southwestern peoples from Late Archaic through Late Basketmaker times. As the early Puebloans abandoned the pithouse as a living space, some, but not all, retained it as the kiva. Some kivas were of square design to accommodate local space and materials, but all incorporated the basic elements — a sipapu, firepit ventilator shaft, and roof entry. Large kivas were being constructed along the San Juan River in southeastern Utah about 1,300 years ago. The kiva is central to many modern-day pueblo societies.

wooden or sandstone slab door. The impressions of corn cobs and hands are often found on the finished surfaces.

Prior to the use of above-ground pueblos, people lived in subterranean pithouses. Twelve hundred years ago, when the farmers began opting for the surface roomblock, the family pithouse was often converted into a kiva. These circular underground rooms were the domain of men and the epicenter of spiritual, social, and economic forces within the Kayenta, Mesa Verde, and Chacoan traditions. Eastward into the old Puebloan heartland, kivas were commonplace. They are less common at Grand Canyon. Kiva religion is virtually absent from the Virgin and Cohonina traditions, nor was it practiced by the Fremont or Sinagua. The Hopi and Zuni along with many other Pueblo societies still preserve this old religion.

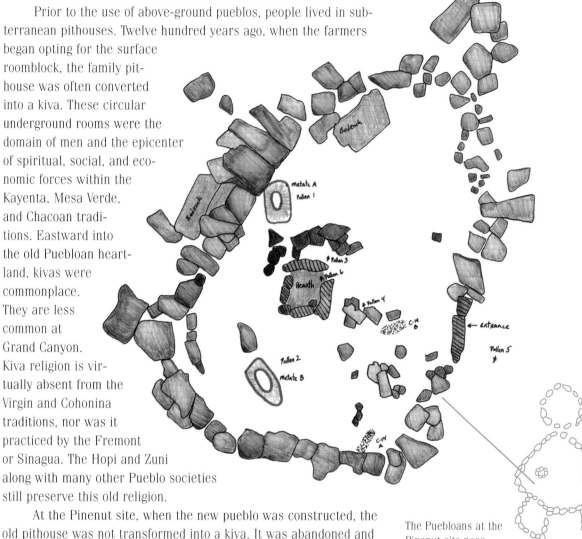

At the Pinenut site, when the new pueblo was constructed, the old pithouse was not transformed into a kiva. It was abandoned and in fact used by the inhabitants for a time as a trash dump. The potentially obsessive piety and zeal which spread outward from Chaco Canyon may have been considered as so much inconvenience to the Cohonina and Virgin farmers working the rocky canyons far to the west. It is also possible these borderland farmers used aboveground structures that are no longer present for religious purposes. The enigmatic stone walls overlooking the river at Cardenas Canyon,

The Puebloans at the Pinenut site near Kanab Canyon had a single room devoted to living space. The rest served as storage, with a shaded work area attached to the south end.

Hilltop Fort at Cardenas Canyon.

known as the Hilltop Fort, may have been such a site.

A formal kiva can be seen at Bright Angel Pueblo, the same site observed by Major John Wesley Powell in 1869. It is situated just downstream from the upper bridge that connects the south side of the canyon to the facilities at Phantom Ranch.

TUSAYAN RUIN

By the late 1100s prehistoric Puebloans in the canyon region were "grouping up" into extended communities rather than living on family farmsteads. The pueblo we call Tusayan, sitting just one-quarter mile south of the canyon rim near Desert View, is a good example of community land use in an arid climate. Park archaeologist Jan Balsom says "... the location was excellent. There were neighbors, nice views of the sacred peaks, good farming in the drainage below the site, and a wide variety of options for hunting and gathering. A trail (known today as the Tanner) into the canyon, where subsistence activities could take place, was a short walk away. For trade, the Coconino Basin and rim areas could be easily approached from the pueblo."

Tusayan was not built until about A.D. 1185, some thirty-five years after people had begun to withdraw from the canyon in earnest. After twenty years of occupation, the pueblo's thirty or so inhabitants joined the migration south and eastward, leaving their homesite as a testimonial of their movement to a place of permanence.

Prehistoric Puebloan Gardens

Agricultural features common to southwestern farming — terraces, ditches, shallow clay-lined depressions, check dams, and actual garden plots outlined with rock borders — are found throughout the canyon country: Walhalla Glades, Kwagunt Delta, Deer Creek, Pinenut, Cataract (Havasu) Canyon, Tusayan, Pasture Wash, and Basalt Canyon, to name just a few. These features were constructed and maintained to channel and store water as well as to hold the fragile soil in place.

Protected and nurtured, every plot was treated with due reverence as the means by which the farmers could stay in the canyon. Each plot was surrounded by a low rock wall that acted as a passive solar device, preventing frost damage to young plants along the river in early spring and the uplands in early summer. The walls also allowed better retention of moisture and kept organic material from dispersing. Modern Pueblo farmers often plant faster-growing wild food plants with domesticated crops to act as shade for the young seedlings. Amaranth is used in this way by the Hopi.

Prehistoric Puebloan farmers used low rock walls to slow erosion.

If the canyon can be defined in any singular fashion, it is as a monumental engine of erosion. Slowing even the smallest increment of erosion is an act of human defiance in the face of adversity. Ultimately, the canyon wins this battle. Nevertheless maintenance of the soil is key to successful farming at Grand Canyon — no soil, no corn. So the old Puebloans spent a lot of time tending their plots. When the soil began to erode in significant amounts 850 years ago, quite notably so did Puebloan culture.

WATER SOURCES

Every water source — seasonal seeps, springs, sandstone tanks — would have been part of each person's mental map, along with trails and every other important resource. Water knowledge made up part of the unwritten cultural lexicon known and understood by each member of the community, young and old alike. Dying of thirst in Grand Canyon is a modern phenomenon attributable to the inexperienced, the unskilled, and the unlucky. It is very hard to imagine a Puebloan, Hualapai, or Paiute dying of thirst.

Cliff Spring

Travel and Trade

Commerce was an important facet of life known to all the peoples at Grand Canyon, linking them economically with their neighbors and the world beyond. As the weather in the uplands warmed and the water level in the river dropped after the spring runoff, cross-canyon movement essential for daily chores, and connections and trade within and outside the canyon would resume. Travel through the Inner Gorge along the river is difficult at best. For efficient travel up and down river, movement took place high above the river on the Tonto Platform and Esplanade, which people accessed

The Anasazi Bridge

by side canyons. An intricate system of local trails existed in the canyon long before the backpacking craze of the twentieth century. Modern trails mimic old prospecting routes that followed older native routes.

Some old trails can still be seen. The trail originating on the bench above Basalt Delta linked this settlement with larger villages downstream at Unkar Delta and Furnace Flats. Others are the old Hopi Salt Trail, the trail to a hematite mine below Parashant Canyon, and the maze of trails traveled by the Hualapai and Southern Paiute. When Hopi guides led Spaniards to the edge of the abyss in 1540, it was to a place where no trails were visible from the rim, the Salt Trail in particular.

People expedited local travel by taking direct routes from point to point. On the north side of the river, upstream from President Harding Rapid, remnants of a Puebloan footbridge, constructed from driftwood sticks, span a gap high in the cliff face. This precarious structure allowed local farmers to scale a thousand-foot bluff and get to the rim quickly. (Today no access is allowed to the site. Known as the Anasazi Bridge, the remarkable feature can be seen from the river.) Other such examples were observed by U.S. Army expeditions of the 1850s in the west end of the canyon. Simple forked-stick ladders connected ledges and systems of benches that would otherwise require several hours to walk around.

At first glance the river seems to be an insurmountable barrier, but is in actuality only a formidable obstacle which people overcame. The exact method of the wet commute is not known, but it apparently happened without much trouble. (Animals do it daily. Deer are commonly seen making the crossing. A three-foot rattlesnake was observed in mid-channel two miles above Lava Falls, bee-lining to the north bank.) During many years, water levels would have been low enough to cross on foot from August through the following March. Other years, when late snowmelt in the Rockies created prolonged runoff, or an intense monsoon caused unpredictable late summer flooding, options for crossing the river would have been more limited.

Trade items coming into the canyon were exotic and diverse: complete vessels from the east, shell bracelets and slate beads from the south, shell beads from the Pacific Coast, and projectile points made by the Fremont. Routes of trade ran upstream to southern Utah and the drainages of the San Juan River. Redware pots made a thousand years ago in the vicinity of Bluff, Utah, are found in Grand Canyon. Shell bracelets made by the Hohokam in far southern Arizona were shaped from mollusks that had lived in the Gulf of California. Macaws from Mexico are found as far north as Westwater Canyon in Utah, carried by traders walking Puebloan roads.

Before the reintroduction of the horse to the American Southwest by the Spanish in 1540, all American Indians, not just those people of the Grand Canyon, traveled on foot. Oral stories tell of migration centuries ago when the Arikara coming down from the north encountered the Grand Canyon before fish-hooking over the Rockies and out onto the Great Plains. The Hopi culture hero Tiyo floated down the Colorado through the canyon to the sea, returning with new songs and instructions for the Snake Dance. There are dozens of stories like these. Being on foot did not hinder the rapid movement of people and goods over vast distances. The Kiowa recount a celebrated raid from Kansas all the way to Supai in Grand Canyon in the 1820s, but this was done on horseback.

The feathers of tropical birds raised or captured in Mexico were one of a variety of trade items brought to the canyon.

Puebloan Exit

By 850 years ago the cycle of increased rainfall that had instigated the Puebloan cultural flourish was reversing itself. The dry
times were coming back. The Colorado River began stripping away
the terraces so conducive to farming, and by 800 years ago there
was not enough sediment-rich flooding each spring to counter the
loss. This unabated erosion led in turn to a critical drop in the local
water table, further reducing the number of acres that could be
planted. Continued farming under drought conditions concentrated
salts in the remaining soil, and each successive harvest left more

Time and erosion have uncovered tools and utensils that
were left by Puebloan peoples
as they moved away from the
canyon.

empty granaries. By 750 years ago there
was not enough rain to support a tenable
crop on the rims. The northwestern fringes
of Pueblo civilization precariously situated at
Grand Canyon were the first to fold under
the early stages of the regional drought
which ultimately affected all of the farming
people of the Southwest.

As we know from earlier examples, this
kind of change in the environment is not necessarily fatal to a culture, but it is directive.
Once again, the locals were forced to make
decisions or have decisions made for them.
This applied to all the inhabitants of the
canyon, from Glen Canyon through the Grand
Wash Cliffs. The farther west in the canyon
one travels, the harsher the climate and the
quicker the drought would have had an
effect. After two years of an extended
drought, reserve and stored supplies of corn
would dwindle. Every crop would be marginal and the carrying capacity of the land
diminished in proportion. At their maximum
population growth, the villages were looking
into the face of a drought that would last longer than they could
stay. Sadly, the old and the young would die first. Malnutrition,
diseases of deficiency, and starvation stalked the villages. By 850
years ago (A.D. 1150) environmental change and unseen social

pressures had driven the Cohonina off the canyon rim toward the Flagstaff area.

The Kayenta villagers hung on in dwindling numbers for a few generations, until about A.D. 1230. During this final Puebloan phase at Grand Canyon they constructed several thick-walled, seemingly defensive fortlike structures along the south rim between Zuni Point and the Great Thumb. So there could well have been considerable tension and fear brought by the hunger accompanying the drought. Was the caution prompted by the ancestral Hualapai/Havasupai moving upstream, or advance parties of Southern Paiute on the north rim or other displaced Puebloans? We can't really say. As times grew leaner it would have been easy to rationalize taking what was needed from those who had a surplus, unless of course there was a rule against such behavior. It was from these hard and dry times the Zuni people developed the practice of never harming people who grow maize. This may be an insight as to how local alliances sorted themselves out on the Puebloan frontier. By A.D. 1250 localized warfare and regional raiding were taking place across the American Southwest.

The manifestations of long-term drought were felt not only at the table. They were destructive to the intricate fabric of culture beyond an individual's view. With the routine of daily life and familiar cycle of the seasons disrupted, more time was devoted to gathering wild foods, leaving less time for the old chores and rituals. The

During Puebloan times, an alluvial terrace attached this bedrock bench and its group of four rooms to the river. Erosion after A.D. 1200 removed the sediment and left isolated blocks of limestone.

RETURNING FRAGMENTS OF THE PAST

In 1990 the Native American Graves Protection and Repatriation Act (NAGPRA) was signed into law in order to expedite the return of all native skeletal remains and grave goods to the appropriate tribe(s) and to foster a sense of respect for American Indian remains.

"Prehistoric" human remains are rare at Grand Canyon. Literally, only a handful of skeletal materials have been found, telling us virtually nothing. The Havasupai and Hualapai cremated their dead, accounting for a lack of remains from that quarter.

The prehistoric Pueblo generally disposed of the deceased by expedient burial in the trash midden outside the pueblo. High-status and special-circumstance burials are common to the prehistoric Puebloan world, but are yet to be uncovered in the canyon.

web of trade was broken, and kinship ties outside the canyon harder to maintain. The news carried on the lips of the traders was gone with the pots they carried on their backs.

Even in the face of such hardship, life at Grand Canyon went on. Corn was still grown. Tusayan Pueblo on the south rim near Desert View was not even built until eight hundred years ago and was occupied for at least a generation (A.D. 1175 to 1230). In the river gorge and on the south rim, we find small quantities of Pueblo ceramics made less than seven hundred years ago. There is no evidence of a single mass exodus from the canyon. Populations shrank the same way they had expanded in the eleventh century: quickly at first, followed by a slow dribble of departures. The true death blow to the old Puebloan cultures came three centuries later when the Spanish conquest brought enslavement, Catholicism, and European disease.

HOPI TIES

Twenty-three Hopi clans trace their origins to Grand Canyon. In particular, the Bear Strap, Greasy Eye Socket, and Bluebird clans migrated out of the Little Colorado gorge. They tell a tale of three groups of people leaving the canyon in turn. As they topped the rim, each group in succession encountered a dead bear in increasing states of decay. The first group out observed a rotting bear; the second, an all-but-decomposed one; the third saw bluebirds perched on the scattered bleached white bones. If oral tradition can be trusted to reflect a sequence of events, we can visualize these three clans coming out of the canyon in two years or less.

Some families undoubtedly left early, when it became apparent the drought would persist. Others stayed, readjusting in their own way. Small pockets of Virgin branch people isolated on the north side in the canyon's far west end toughed it out, relying on the food they could gather, planting in nooks and crannies, having fewer children, and going lighter on the calories.

Once again the wheel was turning. At some point around 775 years ago (A.D. 1225), village life on the deltas in eastern Grand Canyon and on the forested rims became untenable and the final Puebloan families moved out of the canyon. These people chose to leave their homes due to circumstances beyond their control, but not beyond their understanding. They emerged into a world with a

peaking population and an ominous drought. So with their farming heritage and what goods they could carry, they walked out of the canyon into an increasingly dry and hostile world toward the Hopi mesas and points south: Wupatki, the Little Colorado, and the well-watered Verde Valley. The Hopi Mesas acted as a refugium for corn-growing Uto-Aztecan speakers cast out on the landscape during the drought that occurred between 600 and 800 years ago. It was these groups of Puebloans along with clans from Fremont country, people to the west, and survivors from Casas Grandes in Mexico that amalgamated through necessity over the next few centuries as the Hopi people.

Throughout the last millennium and into modern times the Hopi have maintained their ancient connections to the canyon, ritually in the kivas on the Hopi mesas and physically by trekking to the canyon to collect salt and visit the Sipapuni, an elevated hot spring sacred to specific clans of Hopi, representing their point of origin into this world and their destination when they depart. Hot, iron-rich waters evaporate around the lip of the rounded opening, depositing a rind of earthy yellow pigment used in ritual.

Several years ago I walked with a small group of Hopi priests and elders to this quiet place. They said the world was dying and were focused on reversing this trend through ceremony. After the observance, several of the men packed the thick yellow pigment into white gym socks. We walked the next few hours back to the camp without saying much and over the next several days did not speak of it again. This solemn act was the continuum of a cultural string running back ten centuries to the time when the ancestors of these men and their families lived in the canyon. Hopi do not go into the canyon lightly. They prepare for a trip months in advance. Still farmers, they leave nothing to chance.

On an obscure ledge overlooking Lava Falls Rapid there is an unusual pictograph panel consisting of three Kachina figures. It is curious because the Pueblo people had for the most part moved out of the canyon before the Kachina religion made its way onto the plateau. This panel reminds us that small groups of Puebloans, probably Hopi traders, were returning to this particular place in the canyon. They had moved on, but old ties and new business were bringing them back.

The Sipapuni is the place of origin for the Hopi clans that emerged from Grand Canyon.

AT HOME IN THE CANYON

As Puebloan populations dwindled between 700 and 850 years ago, other cultures were moving to the canyon. From the Mojave Desert came the Cerbat/Pai to inhabit the western end of the canyon, south of the Colorado River. Paiute migrated southward from the Great Basin of Nevada and Utah and stopped north of the Colorado. Though the two cultures arrived at the canyon at about the same time, they were unrelated.

The Cerbat/Pai

The Cerbat/Pai, direct ancestors of the Hualapai and Havasupai, arrived at the canyon with low-desert skills that would allow them to flourish where the farmers could no longer be sustained. For centuries they had traded with

Early camps of the Cerbat/Pai would have looked much like this. The presence of tin cans is practically the only distinguishing feature of this Havasupai camp photographed by George Wharton James in 1900.

the Puebloans from their home territory in the canyon's west end, but the archaeological record does not clearly reveal when they occupied the entire river corridor as permanent residents.

Some scholars believe the Cerbat/Pai entered the canyon a century after the prehistoric Pueblo left, but the Cerbat were moving up-canyon in reaction to the same drought that was plaguing the Puebloan farmers and were probably on the move even before the Puebloan withdrawal. Other researchers believe the newcomers pushed the prehistoric Pueblo out by force. Scattered warfare and raids were inevitable. The Kayenta Puebloans built enigmatic defensive structures along the south rim during this period of flux. Conflict, when it took place, would have been on a limited scale. Small groups of people were drifting in and out of the region, not large armies. That, of course, makes the experience no less intense for the participants. It is also feasible that the few Puebloans who refused to leave taught their ways of farming to the Cerbat/Pai and simply were absorbed. It is most plausible the majority of Puebloans were not driven out at the tip of an arrow, but prodded by an empty fork.

The Hualapai origin myth directs us to Mada Widita Canyon (Meriwitchica on the maps) in the extreme west end of Grand Canyon. There, in Wahavo, a pueblo built in a cave high up on the canyon wall, lived their culture hero Kathat Kanave, an old man and sometimes-coyote, who taught them the proper way to live. He told them what and when to plant, how to resolve disputes, what medicines could be found in the canyon and other singularly Puebloan information, a pretty clear indication that some overlap existed between the two cultures though the physical record shows scant evidence.

Cerbat/Pai archaeological sites are very different from prehistoric Puebloan sites. Yet, in the canyon's west end there is amalgamation of the old and the new. Good flat places to live are at a premium in the canyon and over the centuries a good spot often remains the only spot; so where it occurs, it is occupied. Artifacts blend together on the surface causing anxiety for the archaeologist. Tizon Brownware pottery is a trait of the Cerbat, originating at sites on the lower Colorado River and produced with little change between 1,200 and 250 years ago. The Cerbat/Pai manufactured it prior to their movement eastward into Grand Canyon proper. Sherds of Tizon Brownware have been found far upstream at Unkar Delta on Puebloan sites dating to a thousand years ago.

The Cerbat/Pai moved in an established rhythm from water source to water source, hunting deer and bighorn sheep, gathering mesquite, prickly pear, their staple agave (mescal), and other plant foods. Barely discernable short-term camps typically would consist of very few artifacts: a cleared circular area and rock ring where a gowa, a brush shelter, had stood, a small roasting pit, some hand-held tools, a grinding slab or anvil stone, a few scattered flakes, an occasional Tizon sherd. Less often there might be a Littleman point or a fragment of a Hopi tradeware pot. Such a minimalist site represents a family on its traditional rounds, utilizing specific resources along the rims and river as seasons dictated.

More complex long-term camps existed under the shelter of the rims and down along the river where side canyons open into the gorge. These were the home bases of extended families, where evidence of use over multiple generations, perhaps centuries, is found: overlapping conical roasting pits twenty feet in diameter and seven feet high, pictographs, digging sticks, broken pots, quids of chewed-and-spat-out mescal fibers, all the debris of daily life that time has not engulfed. Common in western Grand Canyon are low rock walls next to game trails, used by hunters as points of ambush for bighorn sheep.

The Cerbat/Pai traded, exporting deer hides and dried meat, sheets of mescal, and highly valued red hematite *(gwat)* in buckskin bags, which moved eastward through the Hopi and west as far as Baja California, in exchange for Hopi and Mojave pottery, woven goods, and, closer to our own time, gunpowder, brass, and rifles.

Six hundred years ago the Cerbat/Pai were the dominant tribe along the south rim of Grand Canyon from the mouth of the Bill Williams River below Hoover Dam, up to the confluence of the Little Colorado. Divided up into eleven or twelve geographically determined bands including the Havasupai, they represented a confederation that spoke the same language, shared a heritage and an inherited landscape, and lived in what eminent Grand Canyon archaeologist Dr. Robert Euler aptly describes as territorial equilibrium.

In 1994 while I was driving on Hualapai Reservation 150 miles west of Grand Canyon Village with tribal archaeologist Man Susanyatame, a Hualapai descended from the Pine Springs band, I asked him how he thought those families living down along the river kept in touch with the rest of their people. He said, "It was the runners. The Giv' iyam. All they did was run. They carried the news . . . they got everything they needed from the people for bringing the news." Kept informed by the Giv' iyam, the bands could mobilize quickly against a common enemy or come together for rabbit drives and dances.

The Havasupai, centuries back, had made lifestyle decisions based on local circumstances and were headed along a different track than the other Hualapai bands. They more or less permanently inhabited Cataract Canyon, one of Grand Canyon's largest side canyons and the old homeground of the Cohonina. Before 1875 the Havasupai (Nyava Kopai) were the easternmost band of the Hualapai Confederation. Because they maintained gardens and

Early peoples used split green-wood tongs to collect the fruit of prickly pear cactus. Singeing the spines or using a rabbit-foot brush to rub them off, they ate the fruit fresh or split and dried it for storage.

lived half of the year in Cataract Canyon, the U.S. Army considered them distinct from the Hualapai. Thus they were spared the brutal Hualapai War (1867–1872) and emerged into the twentieth century recognized by the federal government as a separate tribe. Because they were far enough west, they reversed the delta farmers' tactics and wintered comfortably in the uplands. As the agave ripened they moved down, spending planting time through harvest in the canyon bottom where the gardening was good and the sun less intense.

The Hualapai call the Colorado River Hakataia. From the rim, the rapids and endless current seemed to them to be like an animal, alive, the flowing water, its backbone, or *haitat.* Today the Hualapai and Havasupai Reservations extend only from Cataract Canyon to Lake Mead, occupying the forested rim country down to the river for more than a hundred miles. They were pushed out of this lean country, not by a change in the weather, but by greed for gold and the railroad's need for land, timber, and water.

The Southern Paiute

The Paiute hunter-gatherers entered into a country on the north side of the Colorado River that had been the sparsely populated home of the Virgin Puebloans, and here and there isolated farmers were still hanging on, such as at Pinenut and settlements around Mt. Trumbull. It is probably from these residual groups of Puebloans that the first wave of Paiute learned how to supplement their wild foods with corn and squash grown around springs and down in the side canyons.

Southern Paiute and Cerbat/Pai sites are often hard to differentiate based solely on artifacts. A rule of thumb for the Grand Canyon is "Paiute north bank, Cerbat/Pai south bank," but this only works in general. Like the Pueblo groups before them, the Southern Paiute utilized both sides of the river as necessity dictated. During the mid-1800s, Mormon settlement of the Arizona Strip and north rim forced bands of Southern Paiute to seek shelter across the river with their neighbors. Before the Mormons came, the canyon afforded protection from Mountain Ute, Navajo, and Spanish slavers who roamed and raided in the region. Similarly, the government's

The distinctive style of Paiute pictographs is evident through-out the Grand Canyon river corridor.

war against the Hualapai (1867–1872) drove families and bands deeper into the canyon and occasionally north across the river onto Paiute ground.

To the Southern Paiute, the entire Grand Canyon country is a land of power. The specific name of the canyon is Pipaxa' uipi, Big River Canyon. They are great singers, and in song they describe and commemorate their relationship to Grand Canyon. Songs are differentiated into those that pertain to the trails of the living and those that individuals sing to guide themselves on the trail to the afterlife. Like the Hualapai, the Southern Paiute had a guild of runners who carried messages from camp to camp coded into knotted strings called *tapitcapi.* The Southern Paiute cultural landscape was held together by a complex system of trails connecting the far-flung water sources in Grand Canyon. The web of trails spreading out across the surface of the Paiute world was committed to memory by song. Because of summer heat or the need to deliver an urgent message, runners moved through the cool night guided by a song that had been passed down through generations. (This information, gathered from modern Paiute people, illustrates how limiting it can be to explain an intricate way of life by just studying broken pottery and arrow points. When this system of organized communication is applied to the past, it adds a little flesh and motion to the texture of Paiute society.)

As with their predecessors and contemporary neighbors, rock art was an important form of expression to the Paiute. A term the Paiute use is *tumpituxwinap,* inadequately translated as storied rocks. Another term is *tumpim po'okant,* roughly meaning having a lot to tell on the rocks. When the glyphs and graphs cannot be deciphered because the symbols come from another culture or are the work of a shaman, they are referred to as *navastump,* nonsense rock. It is assumed the symbols have some specific meaning, but that meaning is lost to the viewer. One of the last Paiute pictograph panels to be executed in Grand Canyon details a Ghost Dance held down along the river in the 1880s. This religious movement was the inspiration of Wovoka, a Northern Paiute man who, after becoming discouraged with Christianity, envisioned the immediate demise of Euroculture and the disappearance of the federal government brought about by repeated staging of the Ghost Dance by all Native

In 1869 explorer John Wesley Powell and his hungry men pillaged the unattended Paiute gardens along the river to enhance their pathetic diet of rancid bacon, flat biscuits, and black coffee. The immature greens made the entire crew violently ill.

Americans. Sadly it culminated in the massacre at Wounded Knee.

The Southern Paiute efficiently gleaned a living from spare land. It was not a shift in the climate or ecological catastrophe that pushed the Paiute out of the canyon, but the expansion of European-American culture into the region from 1850 to 1880. A lifestyle that existed for more than six hundred years in a true balance with the available resources was exterminated in a single generation. Several hundred archaeological sites at Grand Canyon mark its passing. Modern Paiute people live on small reservation lands north of Grand Canyon proper in Arizona, Utah, and Nevada.

A SOURCE OF POWER

For American Indians, there is an important connection between spiritual power and place. The Southern Paiute call sites of traditional significance *pohaghani,* houses of power. At Grand Canyon there are numerous examples associated with several cultures: the Sipapuni, Ribbon Falls, the Salt Cave, Deer Creek Falls, Three Springs, and countless others, forgotten or not spoken of.

Several aspects of the power that resides in the natural world come together at the mouth of Prospect Canyon, the site of Lava Falls Rapid. Here the transition from high desert to low desert becomes apparent. Along the river, vegetation changes to ocotillo, barrel cactus, and mesquite. The rim elevations drop. The ponderosa

pine forest gives way to juniper breaks, groves of stunted oak, sage flats, and expanses of barren rock. Dormant volcanoes and cinder cones protrude, and deeply incised canyons carve into the uplands.

At least seven times before humans arrived at Grand Canyon, lava cascaded over the rim at this point and flowed, steaming, down the river channel, cooling into natural dams that pooled the river into large,

elongated lakes for thousands of years at a stretch. Each time, the river wore most of the lava away, but some remained locked to the canyon walls, creating towering jointed cliffs.

In the middle of the Colorado River a mile above Lava Falls, a residual plug of basalt creates an imposing black island which today is known as Vulcans Anvil. The Hualapai call it *wi- nyak-da-lupa,* the big black rock. They, along with the Havasupai and the Southern Paiute, consider the big black rock and surrounding landscape sacred.

"... It's a notion, no more. But some place in the scheme of things this world must touch the other."
— Cormac McCarthy, *Blood Meridian,* 1985

CONCLUSION

The fragments of individual lives and their greater cultures lie scattered on the surface and buried within Grand Canyon. Those broken pots, dormant tools, concentrations of charcoal, and hand-drawn symbols allow us a mist-covered portal into history. Archaeological sites rarely preserve a moment frozen in time. More correctly, sites represent a composite of hours or days or years of activity, partially preserved and thus partially understood.

From studying archaeological sites at Grand Canyon, we can conclude this much: Grand Canyon is unforgiving. The more reliance a culture places on altering the environment to maintain its standard of living, the shorter is its story. There is not a shred of compromise built into the system. Like the geological history of the earth revealed in the walls of the canyon, the various cultures exist in a greater context. Complicated further by the intangible nuances of the human mind, the sites represent more than artifacts can express.

The whole canyon and everything in it is sacred to us, all around, up and down. — Rex Tilousi, Havasupai Elder

During the 1930s, by total coincidence, a group of young Paiute from the north rim and a group of young Hualapai from the south rim simultaneously worked their way down to the basalt-lined benches overlooking Lava Falls. Separated by the river, each group built a large fire and celebrated. They yelled back and forth across the divide, but nobody could make out what was said and nothing else came of it. Forty years later at a more official function, a Paiute woman began talking about the Grand Canyon, its importance to her people, and the bonfire she attended. In the assembled group was a Hualapai woman who had been dancing on the opposite bank. It was an unexpected reunion. The water in the canyon is still dividing and bringing people together.

INDEX

SUGGESTED READING

Cordell, Linda S. and George J. Gumerman, editors, *Dynamics of Southwest Prehistory*, 1989, Smithsonian Institution Press.

Fontana, Bernard L., *Entrada, The Legacy of Spain and Mexico in the United States*, 1994, Southwest Parks and Monuments Association.

Plog, Stephen, *Ancient Peoples of the American Southwest*, 1997, Thames & Hudson.

Riley, Carroll L., *Rio del Norte: People of the Upper Rio Grand from Earliest Times to the Pueblo Revolt*, 1995, University of Utah Press.

Schwartz, Douglas W., *On the Edge of Splendor: Exploring Grand Canyon's Human Past*, 1989, School of American Research.

Walker, Steven L., *The Southwest: A Pictorial History of the Land and its People*, 1993, Camelback Design Group and Canyonlands Publications.

PHOTOGRAPHY CREDITS

Kim Besom 20 right, 21t right; Chris Coder 20t, 21b both, 45, 51, back cover upper left; Marcelle Coder 56; Lois Ellen Frank 22; George H.H. Huey 1, 4, 11, 19, 20 pigments, 28, 34 sherds, 43, 50, 54, back cover lower left; Gary Ladd 21t left, 38, 42, back cover right; Museum of Northern Arizona 31, NA6887.15; NPS 8b, 10, 12, 16, 18, 32, 34 (pot), 40, 41, 48; Northern Arizona University, Cline Library 8t, NAU.PH.98.70; School of American Research, Douglas W. Schwartz 9, 30, 47; Utah Museum of Natural History, University of Utah, Laurel Casjens 26 both; Lisa Whisnant 44.

ILLUSTRATION CREDITS

Roy Andersen, *Daily Life at Tusayan Pueblo*, cover, 36, courtesy of the artist; Chris Coder 28, 39; C. R. Knight (under the direction of Chester Stock) 14; Susan Leach 13, 53; Elizabeth McClelland 41; William Morrow & Company, Inc. cover (pot, ladle, figurine), 3; NPS 20-21; Joe Pachak 16 (points), 19, 23; School of American Research cover (site plan, Unkar Delta), 9 (site plan, Bright Angel); Thames & Hudson Ltd. 17.

t=top; b=bottom of page
Individual photographers and artists hold copyrights to their work.

ABOUT THE AUTHOR

Chris Coder has worked as an archaeologist on the Great Plains and Colorado Plateau since 1980. He spent seven years as a project archaeologist at Grand Canyon National Park and is now archaeologist for the Yavapai-Apache Nation. He earned his Bachelor of Arts degree from Augustana College and his Master of Arts from Northen Arizona University. Chris lives with his wife, Marcelle, and their two daughters near Flagstaff, Arizona.